JENNY BRISTOW

COOKS

gloriously **good** food

JENNY BRISTOW

COOKS

gloriously good food

THE
BLACKSTAFF
PRESS

BELFAST

IN ASSOCIATION WITH UTV

contents

Gloriously Good Food is about real home cooking. Like the television series, the book is for those who enjoy food that's fresh, healthy and full of goodness. The recipes are quick and simple and can be easily adapted to suit everyone's needs. Whether you are cooking for a family, planning a special meal for friends, or just fancy a bit of a treat, there's something here for you. I have also included some good recipes for anyone managing on a tight budget or trying to lose a bit of weight, and there's even a Kids Corner for aspiring young cooks.

With a wider variety of foods now available, we have become much more adventurous about what we cook. We are also more flexible about *when* we eat. The pressures of everyday life mean that more of us are on the go and snacking has become part of our daily routine. *Gloriously Good Food* is packed with suggestions for snacks, salads and sandwiches. For the inexperienced and the very busy there's also a No Cook Corner, which contains simple recipes that can be prepared in minutes.

Nowadays, most of us try to avoid those foods which really don't do us a lot of good. With that in mind, I have used low fat ingredients in many of the recipes and have cut down on things like salt, cream and butter where possible. Cooking methods too have changed, allowing us to get the best from our food. Steaming is a good alternative to boiling and deep fat frying has become, for many of us, a thing of the past. As you will see from the recipes, the end results are every bit as tasty but lower in calories and far better for you. Of course, everyone gives in to temptation once in a while, so I have included a few deliciously wicked alternatives for those weaker moments!

Cooking gloriously good food is my passion and I really enjoy being able to share that. I am now settled in my new kitchen, a converted barn of all things! It is a wonderful place to cook and we've used it as a location for the television series. I hope the recipes here inspire you and show you new and exciting ways of cooking. Don't be afraid to experiment or to adapt the recipes to suit you. After all, cooking should be about enjoying food and having fun!

Jenny Bristow

herbs

Herbs can work wonders in any dish and it's well worth getting to know how and when to use them. I think fresh herbs work best and it's hard to beat the aroma of herbs cut fresh from your own garden, tub or pot. Not everyone has the time to grow herbs, though, and you will find a wide variety at your local supermarket or greengrocer.

Dried herbs are an excellent standby, and have a better and truer flavour if used within six months of purchase – they can often lose their colour and flavour if stored too long. I find that mixing dried herbs with a little olive oil before cooking helps to sharpen their flavour.

Freezer herbs are also a great substitute for fresh herbs and can be found in the freezer compartment of your local supermarket. The colour and flavour are excellent though only the more popular varieties are available. Puréed herbs come in tubes and can also be very convenient if you are busy.

my favourite herbs

coriander

This rather bitter-tasting herb with its fragile pungent leaves is widely used around the world. It is a member of the carrot family and is sometimes called Chinese parsley or cilantro. It is widely used in Indian, Thai and oriental cooking and adds tremendous flavour to spiced dishes. Coriander seeds have a totally different flavour. They are tiny dark brown seeds, with a gentle citrus perfume and, not to confuse you, they are a spice. To use coriander, either use the leaves whole or chop coarsely.

lemongrass

This is an aromatic herb, originating in south-east Asia. It has a lovely citrus flavour with a woody stem which needs peeling and should then be chopped or sliced. Good in rice, with fish, or in Chinese and Thai food.

parsley

One of the more widely used herbs, especially since traditional parsley has now been joined by the Italian flat leaf parsley which is readily available in most supermarkets. Both types of parsley should be chopped before use, though I love the appearance of the larger flat leaf parsley used as a garnish. All herbs, but especially parsley, act as a seasoning as well as a flavouring and you will discover in time that in recipes where this herb is used you can leave out the salt. Good in all savoury dishes.

dill

This is a fragrant herb with light, feathery fronds. It is very delicate and has a sharp, yet sweet flavour. Dill is excellent with fish, green salads and raw vegetable salads. Medically, it is a calming herb and is one of the main ingredients in gripe water which was given to babies. I used to love it and rarely had the hiccups!

thyme

There is a wide family of thyme and each variety has its own distinctive leaf and flavour. It is quite a woody herb and usually the leaves are stripped from the stems before using. If whole stalks of thyme are used, for example as a flavouring to cook with a roast, then the stalks should not be served because of their woody nature. Thyme is excellent in stuffings and with roasts and fruit salads.

basil

This pretty looking plant has a special place on my window sill because of its sweet aroma. It has soft green leaves although you can sometimes find an equally aromatic variety with purple leaves. For me basil works best of all if eaten uncooked; tear or shred the leaves carefully so as not to bruise them and add to recipes with tomatoes, potatoes, fish, pasta and mushrooms.

oils and spices

oils

It's hard to beat the flavour of a good extra virgin olive oil in a dressing or as a base for a salsa. Sunflower, grape seed or a light olive oil are, however, better for cooking. Whatever oil you use, my advice is to cut down on quantity; despite the benefits, there are calories in there and generous ones at that. You only need to brush a pan lightly with oil when cooking and often you can get away with none at all.

kaffir lime leaves

These leaves come dried in jars and are widely available in supermarkets. I have rarely seen fresh ones except in specialist stores. The flavour of lime leaves is more aromatic and less astringent than the juice of fresh limes, though the leaves can be bitter if used in large quantities. Like bay leaves, lime leaves are used only for flavour and should not be eaten. They are great in fish recipes.

chillies

Chillies are very fiery little pods that are loosely related to the pepper family. The red ones are usually milder and sweeter than the green ones. Cut the chillies in half lengthways and remove the seeds (this should reduce the heat slightly), then chop up finely. Be careful not to touch your eyes before washing your hands as the heat from the chillies can burn. Often, the smaller the chilli, the hotter it is. Jalapeño chillies are particularly hot. I prefer the flavour of fresh chillies although they can be bought dried. They also come in the form of powder, flakes or sauce. You can buy a variety of chilli-infused sauces such as tabasco sauce and harissa.

ginger

Ginger is a root vegetable – it grows underground. Its flavour is fresh and sharp and it works very well in Chinese dishes. It is very pungent and should only be used in small amounts. Peel and chop very finely or grate or crush in a garlic press. Ginger is best stored in the fridge and should keep for up to two weeks. Powdered ginger is no substitute as it has a totally different flavour.

garlic

This robust member of the onion family is widely used in cooking. To prepare garlic, separate the cloves from the bulb, remove the paper and then either slice, chop or purée. I prefer the flavour of squashed or puréed garlic as it is rather sweeter than that of chopped garlic. If making a dressing, garlic is better squashed to avoid those chunky little pieces which hold their shape so well. For a change, try roasting whole cloves of garlic with the paper still on. With longer, slower cooking the garlic develops a sweeter flavour. To eat, just squeeze the garlic out of its paper.

balsamic vinegar

One of the best ingredients the Italians have sent us. This dark, aged vinegar has a sweet rich flavour that adds something special to whatever you cook. It is ideal for dressings and sauces and wonderful as a marinade. Use it liberally – recipes usually call for two or three dessert spoonfuls – and buy the best you can afford.

stock

If possible try to use fresh stock. Stock cubes, however, work just as well, but be careful of the higher salt content.

conversion tables

volume

1 tsp	5mls
1 dsp	10mls
1 tbsp	15mls
55mls	2floz
75mls	3floz
125mls	4floz
150mls	5floz ($1/4$ pt)
275mls	$1/2$pt
425mls	$3/4$pt
570mls	1pt
1 litre	$1^3/4$pts

oven temperatures

degrees centigrade	gas mark
140°	1
150°	2
170°	3
180°	4
190°	5
200°	6
220°	7
230°	8
240°	9

weights

grams	ounces/pounds
10g	$1/2$oz
25g	1oz
40g	$1^1/2$oz
50g	2oz
60g	$2^1/2$oz
75g	3oz
110g	4oz
125g	$4^1/2$oz
150g	5oz
175g	6oz
200g	7oz
225g	8oz
250g	9oz
275g	10oz
350g	12oz
400g	14oz
450g	1lb
700g	$1^1/2$lbs
900g	2lbs
1.3kg	3lbs

measurements

millimetres	inches
3mm	$1/8$ inch
5mm	$1/4$ inch
1cm	$1/2$ inch
2cm	$3/4$ inch
2.5cm	1 inch
3cm	$1^1/4$ inches
4cm	$1^1/2$ inches
4.5cm	$1^3/4$ inches
5cm	2 inches
7.5cm	3 inches
10cm	4 inches
13cm	5 inches
15cm	6 inches
18cm	7 inches
20cm	8 inches
23cm	9 inches
25cm	10 inches
28cm	11 inches
30cm	12 inches

snacks, salads, starters

At some time most of us will face the dilemma of having to prepare food at a moment's notice. This section provides you with a range of salads and sweet and savoury snacks that are imaginative, quick and relatively low in calories. Most of the recipes will make a light snack on their own but you need only serve them with crusty bread, croutons or even pasta to turn them into a more filling meal. The crusty bread with roasted salmon flakes and basil mayonnaise is delicious or, for those with a sweeter tooth, try the hot sugar cinnamon muffins with apple wedges. If you feel like treating yourself or if you are entertaining, the salad of poached pears, blue cheese and figs or the roasted cherry tomato soup make excellent starters and are vegetarian-friendly.

poached pears, blue cheese and figs
with a walnut dressing

Serves 2

This is one of my favourite starters – fresh pears, a light creamy blue-veined cheese, figs and a few mixed salad leaves. A light dressing made with walnut oil really complements the other flavours in the dish.

2 pears
juice of $^1/_2$ lemon

1 Peel and quarter the pears and toss in a little lemon juice before cooking.

570mls/1pt water
1 dsp caster sugar
1 tsp lemon juice

2 Add the sugar and lemon juice to a saucepan of boiling water. Dissolve the sugar by stirring well. Add the quartered pears to the syrup and poach gently for 4–5 minutes until they just show signs of softening. Remove the pears from the syrup.

75g/3oz soft creamy blue cheese
1 fresh fig – quartered

3 Top the pears with cheese and heat below a hot grill with the figs for 1 minute until the cheese melts and the figs toast slightly.

walnut dressing

2 dsp walnut oil
2 dsp olive oil
2 dsp white wine vinegar
$^1/_4$ tsp mustard
salt and freshly ground black pepper

1 Whisk all the ingredients together until well mixed.

mixed leaves –
e.g. watercress or lamb's lettuce
walnuts

2 Arrange the leaves on a plate. Top with pears, figs, walnuts and spoon over a little dressing just before serving.
To turn this dish into a light lunch, increase the quantities and serve with either crispy bacon or smoked ham.

3

hot fish and potato salad

Serves 4

White fish is so low in fat and easy to cook. In this recipe I have used a new and unusual kind, Antarctic white fish. However, you can easily use cheaper varieties such as haddock and whiting which are both more readily available.

450g/1lb white fish
juice of 1/2 lemon
salt and freshly ground black pepper

1 Cut the fish into cubes. Sprinkle with lemon juice, some salt and black pepper, then steam for 7–8 minutes until tender. Be careful not to overcook the fish.

225g/8oz baby potatoes – unpeeled

2 Steam the baby potatoes until tender (approximately 20 minutes depending on the size).

3–4 spring onions
110g/4oz cherry tomatoes
few sun blush tomatoes
1 leek

3 Chop the spring onions into 1 inch long strips and mix with the tomatoes. Cut the leek into slices.

sauce

2 dsp Worcester sauce
2 dsp honey
1 dsp tomato and chilli sauce

1 Mix the Worcester sauce and honey in a pan. Heat until the sauce bubbles, then add the leeks, spring onions, tomatoes and tomato and chilli sauce. Cook for 2–3 minutes, then add the steamed potatoes and cook well for a further 2 minutes to allow the flavours to come together.

1 sprig parsley

2 Finally add the steamed fish, mix, then garnish with parsley. Taste for seasoning and serve immediately.

garden salad with a green olive dressing

Serves 4

A simple salad made with everyday ingredients which can be served warm or cold.

450g/1lb baby potatoes – halved
225g/8oz sliced green beans
225g/8oz fresh garden peas
small box mustard cress

1 Steam all the vegetables – potatoes for 20–25 minutes, peas and green beans for 2–3 minutes. Add all the vegetables to the bowl along with the cress.

green olive dressing

2 dsp extra virgin olive oil
1 dsp white wine vinegar
1 dsp lemon juice
$^1/_2$ tsp mustard
salt and freshly ground black pepper

2 Mix the ingredients together for 30 seconds, then pour over the vegetables. Dress the salad while hot so that the vegetables will absorb the dressing. Allow to cool, and serve.

7

sweet chilli bok choi
and gai lan

Serves 2–3

Chinese vegetables are delicious and require hardly any preparation. Just wash well before use and be careful not to overcook.

Gai lan (Chinese broccoli) and bok choi can be steamed, boiled or stir-fried. Every part of these vegetables – leaves and stems, and even the buds and flowers on the gai lan, can be eaten. Their flavour is delicate, sweet and succulent and they are best eaten as fresh as possible. If storing, keep in the refrigerator, lightly wrapped in paper for just a few days.

1 bunch bok choi
1 bunch gai lan

Wash the vegetables well and remove any firm stalks from the base of the vegetables. If preferred, the vegetables can be lightly steamed for 2 minutes before stir-frying.

sweet chilli sauce

1 dsp olive oil
1 inch of root ginger – finely chopped
1–2 cloves of garlic – finely chopped
2 spring onions – finely chopped
1/2 red chilli – finely chopped
1/2 green chilli – finely chopped

1 Heat the oil in a wok or pan and add the ginger, garlic, spring onions and chilli. Cook for 2 minutes, stirring often to prevent sticking.

5g/1oz soft brown sugar
4–5 dsp soy sauce

2 Add the brown sugar and soy sauce. Cook for 1 minute, then add the vegetables. Cook for only 2 minutes as the vegetables will wither very quickly. Serve on their own or as an accompaniment.

9

herb crusted cheesy stuffed mushrooms

Serves 2

A tasty filling snack which could also be served as a starter, made with large flat field mushrooms and topped with creamy blue cheese and parsley. Serve with or without breadcrumbs. If you have to wash the mushrooms, do it just before you use them.

4 large flat mushrooms
salt and freshly ground black pepper
2 cloves of garlic – crushed
2 dsp olive oil

1 Place the mushrooms in a roasting dish, season, brush with oil and garlic and roast in the oven @ 200°C/gas mark 6 for 15 minutes.

225g/8oz watercress or spinach

2 Wilt the spinach or watercress by steaming for 1–2 minutes.

110g/4oz creamy blue cheese
e.g. belle bleu or Stilton
1 dsp parsley – finely chopped
4 dsp brown or white breadcrumbs

3 Remove the mushrooms from the oven and top with wilted spinach, cheese, parsley and breadcrumbs.

2–4 slices crusty bread

4 Place under a hot grill along with the slices of bread and cook until the cheese melts, bubbles and browns. Serve the mushrooms on top of the crusty bread.

creamy mushrooms

Another quick idea for mushrooms: toss some assorted mushrooms in a pan with some butter and olive oil for 2–3 minutes. Mix with soured cream and olives and serve piled high on toasted bread.

roasted cherry tomato soup

Serves 4

The flavour of a good homemade soup is hard to beat and today's soups can be uncomplicated affairs. This tomato soup has a wonderfully intense flavour which comes from roasting the tomatoes slowly in the oven.

900g/2lbs cherry tomatoes
salt and freshly ground black pepper
1 dsp olive oil

1   Place the tomatoes in a roasting dish, season, sprinkle with the oil and roast in the oven @ 220°C/gas mark 7 for 15 minutes until softened and blackened. This will improve the flavour. Remove from the oven and whiz in the blender until the tomatoes become puréed.

1 onion – finely chopped
2 cloves of garlic – finely chopped
1 dsp olive oil
handful of basil – chopped
275mls/^{1}/2pt vegetable stock

2   Cook the onion and garlic for 2–3 minutes in a large saucepan with the oil. Add the basil, the blended tomatoes and the vegetable stock. Put a lid on the saucepan and leave to simmer for 15 minutes.

3   Taste and adjust the seasoning if necessary. If the soup is too thick add more stock until it reaches the required consistency.

to serve

As a starter add a spoonful of yoghurt and garnish with some basil leaves.

It makes a great lunch if you add a sandwich, i.e. green olive bread filled with creamy Stilton cheese and cucumber.

13

italian sausage sandwich

Serves 1

Sausages come in all shapes and sizes and are flavoured with different herbs and spices. You should have no bother finding one that you like.

2 sausages

1 Lightly oil a griddle pan and add the sausages. Cook for approximately 7–10 minutes until cooked through.

1 small ciabatta loaf – sliced lengthways

2 Add the bread, cut side down, to the pan and cook for one minute until golden.

2 tomatoes – finely diced
1 dsp tomato passata
1 spring onion – finely chopped
salt and freshly ground black pepper
crispy lettuce leaves
sprig of fresh basil

3 Mix the tomatoes, passata and spring onions in a bowl to form a salsa. Taste and season.

4 Assemble the sandwich by placing a slice of ciabatta on a serving plate. Top with some crispy lettuce and add the sausages and salsa. Garnish with a sprig of fresh basil.

chicken and ham sandwich

Serves 1

Potato bread now comes in so many different flavours and is very versatile. It is ideal to use as part of a snack or a sandwich.

1 chicken fillet

1 Chargrill the chicken fillets on a griddle pan for approximately 8–10 minutes. The cooking time will depend on the thickness of the fillet.

2 slices ham
1 slice potato bread
few black olives
few sliced tomatoes
1 dsp low fat mayonnaise
sprig of fresh basil

2 Add all the other ingredients to the pan just to heat through for two minutes. Assemble the sandwich by spreading the toasted potato bread with some mayonnaise and continue by layering the chicken, ham, olives and tomatoes. Top with the remainder of the mayonnaise and a sprig of fresh basil.

15

grilled sardine and bacon sandwich
with lemon scented mayo

Serves 1

A quick and very tasty sandwich made with hot grilled sardines, streaky bacon and wholesome wheaten bread.

2 rashers streaky bacon
1 small tin sardines

1 Grill the bacon on a hot griddle pan for approximately 2 minutes, then add the sardines and heat for another minute. Use some kitchen paper to absorb any excess oil.

1–2 tsp lemon juice
2 dsp mayonnaise – low fat
1 slice wheaten bread

2 Mix the lemon juice with the mayonnaise and spread half of it on the wheaten bread. Add bacon and sardines and top with the rest of the lemon mayonnaise.

17

toasted bread, plums, bacon and creamy blue cheese

Serves 1

Use any bread for this snack, either baguettes, soda or Italian bread and top with any variety of bacon and blue cheese.

1 baguette – halved
1 dsp olive oil

2–3 plums – cut into slices
3–4 slices bacon
50g/2oz blue cheese

1 Place the halved baguette, cut side down, on a hot griddle pan which has been brushed with olive oil.

2 Add the sliced plums and bacon to the griddle pan and cook for 2–3 minutes.

3 Turn over the grilled bread and top with cooked plums, bacon and, finally, the cheese.

4 Place under a hot grill for 1 minute until the cheese melts. Serve immediately.

crusty bread with roasted salmon flakes
and a basil mayonnaise

Serves 1

A very tasty snack or sandwich. Roasted salmon flakes are a relatively new product and are available in the chill cabinet in most supermarkets. They are already cooked and so are ideal for quick snacks.

2 dsp low fat mayonnaise
1/2 tsp tabasco sauce
1 dsp tomato paste
1 tsp lemon juice
1 dsp basil – chopped
1 crusty roll – halved

1 Mix the first five ingredients together, then spoon two-thirds of this mixture onto the base of the roll.

110g/4oz roasted salmon flakes
few black olives
1 spring onion – chopped
flat leaf parsley
1 lime – sliced

2 Top with salmon flakes, black olives, spring onions and parsley and garnish with the remainder of the dressing and some slices of lime.

19

irish french toast

Serves 1

Soda bread with its soft, spongy texture makes really good french toast. Here are two ideas for a quick economical snack, one sweet and one savoury, both made with everyday ingredients.

2 eggs
75mls/3floz milk
pinch of salt
1 white soda farl
10g/¹/2oz butter
1 tsp olive oil

1 Break the eggs into a bowl. Whisk along with the milk and a pinch of salt. Cut the soda bread in two and soak in the mixture for 30 seconds.

2 Heat the butter and oil in a shallow frying pan. Add the coated soda bread and cook lightly on either side, turning once. Cooking should take only a couple of minutes in total. Use a little kitchen paper to absorb any excess oil.

serve savoury

2 dsp pickles
2 dsp onion relish
25g/1oz cheese, e.g. Wensleydale

1 Mix the pickles and relish together and spoon onto the toast. Crumble the cheese on top and brown under a very hot grill.

serve sweet

1 red apple
1 green apple
2 plums
1 tsp brown sugar
1 dsp water

1 Core the apples and cut them into wedges, skin still on, and quarter the plums. Gently poach in the water and sugar for approximately 2–3 minutes until soft.

1 dsp yoghurt
sprig of mint

2 Spoon the fruit onto the farl and top with yoghurt. Garnish with a sprig of mint.

21

hot banana muffelletta

Serves 1

The combination of brown bread, banana and nutmeg is delicious. Enjoy this sandwich at any time of the day.

2 slices buttered brown bread
1 tsp brown sugar
$^1/_2$ tsp nutmeg

2 bananas
juice of 1 lemon

1 Butter the bread on both sides and sprinkle with brown sugar and nutmeg.

2 Slice the bananas, toss in the lemon juice and layer them on top of one of the pieces of bread. Place the other slice on top and cook on a griddle pan, turning once, until the banana softens and the bread toasts.

3 Serve with a little yoghurt.

grilled sugar cinnamon muffins
with hot apple wedges

Serves 2

This is a quick and tasty snack for any time of the day or night. The muffins take on an irresistable coating when cooked with the sugar on the hot griddle pan. I prefer to use a combination of red and green apples for colour and crunch.

1 red apple
1 green apple
juice of 1 lemon

1 Cut the apples into wedges and remove the core. Toss in a little lemon juice

25g/1oz melted butter
1 dsp honey

2 Brush the base of a large griddle pan with melted butter and place the apples at one side. Pour a little honey on top of the apples and leave to cook until soft.

25g/1oz demerara sugar
1 tsp cinnamon
2 muffins – savoury or sweet

3 Dust the opposite side of the pan with brown sugar and a hint of cinnamon.

4 Press the muffins down onto the griddle pan to coat them with the sugar and cinnamon and cook for 1 minute on either side until toasted.

vanilla ice cream

Serve the muffins topped with the apples and a spoonful of vanilla ice cream.

25

the main event

The recipes here introduce you to some new dishes and give a few traditional ones a fresh spin. You'll find leg of lamb, always a favourite, but now it is pepper crusted and cooked in half the time with even more flavour. Chicken continues to be the most popular meat we eat, but have you tried it cooked in an aromatic seville orange sauce and served with a pilaff of coriander rice? There's also a middle eastern curry that is full of heat and spice but keeps a hint of sweetness. Fish is very much to the fore in this section, especially with the new varieties that are now available. Try chargrilled marlin served simply on kebabs or tagliatelle with lime scallops. There are also some wonderful vegetable dishes, such as the lemon and olive scented mediterranean vegetables, which are delicious served as accompaniments or make a hearty meal on their own.

Robin Cherry from Carnlea, Ballymena, a local grower of exotic vegetables

seville orange chicken
with a pilaff of coriander rice

Serves 4

Chicken is a great low fat food which absorbs flavours very easily. This aromatic chicken dish is made with that bitter little orange from the south of Spain and a hint of sweet sherry. For a delicious meal serve with a pilaff of coriander rice.

2 cloves of garlic
peel of 1 orange – finely grated
2 tsp cayenne pepper
4 chicken breasts –
110g/4oz each in size

1 Make the dry marinade by pounding together the garlic, orange peel and cayenne pepper. This is most easily done with a pestle and mortar. The process may take a little time but eventually the marinade will become smooth. Spread the marinade evenly over both sides of the chicken fillets. Place in a bowl and cover with cling film. Leave to marinate in the fridge for at least 30 minutes.

2 Add the marinated chicken fillets to a hot dry pan; there should be enough moisture in the marinade to cook the chicken. Cook each side for 2–3 minutes until brown.

150mls/^{1}/4pt sweet sherry
225g/8oz baby onions
2 dsp marmalade
275mls/^{1}/2 pt chicken stock
salt and freshly ground black pepper
2–3 oranges – unpeeled and sliced

3 Next add the sherry, the peeled onions, the marmalade, stock, salt, freshly ground black pepper and sliced oranges.

4 Place the lid on the pan and simmer gently for 25–30 minutes until the sauce has reduced and the chicken has cooked through.

pilaff of coriander rice

^{1}/2 onion – finely chopped
^{1}/2 tsp olive oil
225g/8oz basmati rice
1 dsp coriander – finely chopped
570mls/1pt chicken stock

1 Gently toss the onion in a little olive oil in a large pan until glistening.

2 Add the basmati rice and toss around for 1–2 minutes.

3 Add the fresh coriander.

4 Next add all the stock at once. Stir only once and leave to simmer for about 10–12 minutes until the rice has absorbed the stock and the grains have softened. Garnish with fresh coriander.

pan roasted chicken

with lemon, garlic and herbs

Serves 2

This recipe brings out all the flavour of the chicken by adding lots of seasoning and fresh herbs. An ideal dish to serve with pasta.

8 chicken pieces – drumsticks, wings or thighs
2 cloves of garlic – chopped
1 inch of root ginger – finely chopped
1 tsp cayenne pepper
1 dsp olive oil

1 Mix the garlic, ginger and cayenne pepper in a small bowl – or use a pestle and mortar if you have one – and crush until they form a paste. Heat the oil in a pan and add the paste and the chicken pieces. Cook for 5–6 minutes over a high temperature until the chicken is golden brown.

225g/8oz baby onions or shallots – peeled and halved
1 lemon – cut into slices
juice of 1 lemon
275mls/1/2pt chicken stock
salt and freshly ground black pepper

2 Add the onion and toss with the chicken for 1 minute. Next in with the sliced lemon, the lemon juice, stock, salt and black pepper. Leave to simmer gently for 25 minutes.

pasta

225g/8oz dried pasta
pinch of salt
1 dsp olive oil

3 Bring some water to the boil in a large saucepan. Add the salt and olive oil. When boiling rapidly, add the pasta and cook according to the instructions. Drain and keep warm until you are ready to serve the chicken.

handful of basil – roughly chopped
handful of parsley – roughly chopped

4 Just before serving the chicken, add the herbs. Simmer for 5 minutes to allow the flavours to infuse. Serve with the pasta.

31

garlic and bacon wrapped chicken pieces

Serves 4

Chicken pieces wrapped in bacon and oven roasted with garlic and onions make a delicious snack. This dish is also extremely versatile and for a more substantial meal can be served with pasta, rice, potatoes or toasted bread.

8 chicken drumsticks
8 rashers of streaky bacon
1 dsp olive oil
knob of butter

1   Wrap the bacon around the chicken pieces then brown in a hot frying pan with the oil and butter (the addition of the oil prevents the butter from burning at a high temperature). Turn the drumsticks carefully to achieve an even, golden and crispy texture.

2 cloves of garlic – finely chopped
2 onions – sliced

2   Lower the heat and add the garlic and onions and continue to cook until they also become crispy.

25g/1oz soft brown sugar
4 dsp soy sauce
275mls/¹/2pt vegetable stock

3   Add the sugar, soy sauce and stock. Bring to the boil. Place the contents of the pan in an ovenproof dish and cook @ 180°C/gas mark 4 for 45 minutes to 1 hour.

I love this dish served with hot toasted soda bread that has been drizzled with a little olive oil.

golden chicken bake

Serves 3–4

This tasty chicken dish is made on a shoestring budget. The creamy sauce which accompanies the chicken is made with natural yoghurt to cut down on fat.

450g/1lb chicken – cut into strips
1 tsp olive oil
1 clove of garlic – finely chopped
1 inch of root ginger – finely chopped
1 tsp red chilli – deseeded and finely chopped
1 onion – thickly sliced

4 spring onions – chopped

1 Heat the oil in a non-stick pan, add the garlic, ginger and chilli and cook for 1 minute.

2 Add the chunky pieces of onion and continue to cook for several minutes. Increase the heat and add the chicken strips. Cook for 3–4 minutes, stirring well to prevent the chicken from sticking, until golden brown and lightly cooked.

3 Into the pan with the spring onions. Heat through.

sauce

125mls/4floz chicken stock
1 dsp cornflour
2 dsp cold water
2 dsp natural yoghurt

Now add the chicken stock to the pan. Blend the cornflour with the cold water to stabilise it and mix with the yoghurt. Add this mixture to the pan. The temperature is important in this dish so ensure it remains very low. Allow the chicken to gently simmer in the yoghurt sauce for 5–6 minutes.

pasta

225g/8oz dried pasta
pinch of salt
1 tsp olive oil

In a large saucepan bring some water to the boil. Add a pinch of salt and the olive oil. Add the pasta and cook according to the instructions. Drain well.

110g/4oz grated cheddar cheese

To assemble the dish place the chicken with the yoghurt sauce in an ovenproof dish. Top with the pasta, sprinkle with a little grated cheese and finish by browning under a very hot grill until golden.

tagliatelle with lime scallops

Serves 2

Although available fresh at most fish counters, scallops are also a very useful food to have in your freezer. The more simply they are cooked the better they taste. This idea also works well with prawns, monkfish or with any of the round white fish such as haddock or cod.

2 dsp lime juice
zest of 1 lime
50g/2oz butter

1 Make a lime butter by mixing together the lime juice, zest and butter until soft. Keep to one side until required.

225g/8oz tagliatelle
pinch of salt
1 dsp olive oil

2 In a large saucepan bring some water to the boil. Add a pinch of salt and the olive oil. Add the pasta and cook according to the instructions. When cooked, drain and return to the pan to keep warm. If you wish add a little more olive oil to keep the pasta moist.

8–10 scallops – removed from shell
1 dsp olive oil
1 lime – cut into slices

3 If using frozen scallops, defrost and remove the pink coral. Place on a hot griddle pan lightly brushed with olive oil. Cook for only 2–3 minutes on either side, turning once. The lime slices can be cooked and blackened on the griddle pan at the same time as the scallops are cooking.

handful of parsley or coriander

4 To serve, spoon the pasta onto a dish and place the scallops and the toasted lime slices on top. Drizzle with lime butter and garnish with parsley or coriander.

chargrilled marlin

Serves 4

Marlin is a member of the swordfish family and is quite a robust fish. It is ideal to cook on the barbecue, grill or even oven roast. Some of the more common fish such as monkfish or tuna can also be used in this recipe, but it is always good to find a new fish and one which is easy to cook.

700g/1 1/2lbs fish fillets

Cut the fish into bite-sized cubes.

marinade

juice of 2 limes
2 cloves of garlic – finely chopped
2 dsp olive oil
salt and freshly ground black pepper
8 kaffir lime leaves

1   Mix the first four ingredients in a bowl, then add the cubes of fish. Leave to marinate for 30 minutes, then drain and place the chunks of fish on kebab sticks, alternating each chunk with lime leaves. This makes an attractive garnish and adds flavour to the fish. If using wooden kebab sticks on the griddle pan or barbecue make sure they have been soaked in cold water for an hour beforehand, otherwise they will catch light and burn.

2   Place the kebabs on a hot griddle pan and cook for 5–6 minutes, turning occasionally and brushing with more of the marinade as they cook. When the fish is blackened and tender, remove from the pan and serve.

mackerel mash
with a corn and herb relish

Serves 4

An energy-packed dish of potatoes, oil-rich smoked mackerel and sweetcorn relish. Smoked mackerel is hot-smoked and does not require cooking.

900g/2lbs potatoes – peeled and cut into chunks

1. Boil the potatoes for approximately 20–25 minutes until cooked. Drain and mash quickly while hot. Return to the saucepan to keep warm.

150mls/^{1}/4pt low fat milk
2 dsp olive oil
2 spring onions – roughly chopped
salt and freshly ground black pepper

2. Heat the milk in a small saucepan. Add the olive oil, spring onions, salt and black pepper. Bring to the boil and simmer for 1 minute before adding the mashed potatoes and mix well.

2 smoked mackerel fillets

3. In a bowl flake the smoked mackerel and add the potato mash. Toss lightly.

corn and herb relish

1 small can sweetcorn
4 dsp corn relish
1 dsp chopped herbs – e.g. coriander or parsley

Mix all the ingredients. This relish can be served either hot or cold with the mackerel mash.

cheesy topped smoked haddock

Serves 4

Fish is the finest of fast foods whichever way you cook it and poaching is an economic and healthy method of cooking that lets you infuse the fish with lots of subtle flavours. This dish can be served without the crusty bread for a lighter snack.

570mls/1pt low fat milk
salt and freshly ground black pepper
1 lemon – cut into wedges
4 fillets smoked haddock – undyed, approximately 225g/8oz each in size

1   Put the milk, salt, black pepper, lemon wedges and the fish into a large saucepan. If the fillets are large, fold the tail and top under to make a uniform shape. Cover the pan and poach gently over a low heat for 6–7 minutes until tender but still slightly firm. Don't worry if the milk takes on a slightly curdled effect.

4 slices crusty bread

2   Lightly toast the slices of bread and place in an ovenproof dish.

topping

110g/4oz ricotta cheese
1 egg – lightly beaten
1/2 tsp Worcester sauce
1/2 tsp wholegrain mustard
parsley or chives – finely chopped
2 dsp low fat milk or cream

1   Mix together the ricotta cheese, egg, Worcester sauce, mustard and herbs until smooth. Add the milk or cream to form a smooth paste.

2   Drain the fish and carefully place each piece on top of a slice of toasted crusty bread. Spoon the topping over the fish and bake in the oven @ 200°C/gas mark 6 for 12–15 minutes until crispy and golden on top. Garnish with chopped parsley or chives.

43

lemon and olive scented mediterranean vegetables

Serves 2–3

Mediterranean vegetables can be cooked in many ways. However, I find that oven roasting or chargrilling are two of the nicest ways to cook them, as the vegetables roast, blacken and sweeten as they cook.

1 aubergine
2 courgettes
4–5 vine tomatoes

1　Cut the vegetables into large chunks and place in an ovenproof dish. There is no need to deseed the tomatoes or peel the vegetables. The tomatoes can also be left on the vine for presentation.

4 cloves of garlic – paper on
1 red chilli – deseeded and finely chopped

2　Add the garlic and chilli and mix thoroughly. When garlic is roasted, it develops an intensely sweet flavour. To eat, simply squeeze the garlic out of its skin.

juice of $^1/_2$ lemon
2 dsp olive oil

3　Sprinkle the lemon juice and olive oil over the vegetables.

salt and freshly ground black pepper

4　Season and cook in the oven at 200°C/gas mark 6 for 30–45 minutes until the vegetables are softened, blackened and cooked. Stir them twice while roasting to make sure they are evenly cooked.

oven roasted potatoes and parsnips
with creamy green vegetables and veggie sausages

Serves 4

This recipe is ideal as a vegetarian meal or makes an interesting accompaniment for a meat or fish dish. These vegetables provide a combination of textures and are also really healthy and full of fibre and vitamins.

4–5 parsnips

1 Wash and peel the parsnips, then cut into chunks.

225g/8oz potatoes

2 Wash the potatoes and cut into chunks similar in size to the parsnips. Put both vegetables in a roasting dish.

2 dsp lemon juice
2 dsp balsamic vinegar
salt and freshly ground black pepper

3 Sprinkle with lemon juice, balsamic vinegar, salt and pepper. Cook @ 200°C/gas mark 6 for 25 minutes until the vegetables are crispy and golden. Stir once during cooking time.

225g/8oz broccoli
225g/8oz green beans

4 Steam the broccoli florets and green beans for 5–6 minutes over a low heat until almost ready.

225g/8oz watercress

5 Add the watercress and steam for 20 seconds, then remove from the heat.

2 dsp horseradish sauce
2 dsp fromage frais

6 Mix the horseradish sauce and fromage frais. Place the parsnips, potatoes and green vegetables in a serving dish. Pour the horseradish sauce over the vegetables and garnish with some watercress. Serve either on its own or with sausages.

225g/8oz vegetarian sausages

Cook the sausages either in a pan or below a hot grill for approximately 10 minutes until tender and golden.

parsnip champ

Serves 4

Champ has become very fashionable and it can be made using a variety of ingredients. In this recipe the sweetness of the parsnips complements the flavour of the potatoes.

900g/2lbs potatoes

1 Peel the potatoes and cut into chunks. Boil for 20–25 minutes or until tender.

450g/1lb parsnips

2 Wash and peel the parsnips and cut into chunks. Steam for 15–20 minutes or until cooked through.

3 Drain and mash both vegetables together.

150mls/^{1}/4pt low fat milk
10g/^{1}/2oz butter
2 spring onions – chopped
salt and freshly ground black pepper
knob of butter

4 Gently heat the milk with the butter and chopped spring onions for 1 minute. Mix with the vegetables and season to taste. Should you prefer a creamier mash, feel free to add more milk. Garnish with a knob of butter.

mozzarella topped vegetable tart
with a bacon lattice

Serves 4

Tarts can be so tasty and versatile. This one cuts down on preparation time by using ready-made and ready-rolled shortcrust pastry.

225g/8oz – 1 large sheet – ready-made, ready-rolled shortcrust pastry

1 Use the pastry to line a 23cm/9 inch ovenproof dish and place in the fridge to rest for 30 minutes.

3 large red onions – cut into small wedges
110g/4oz mushrooms – halved
1 dsp balsamic vinegar
salt and freshly ground black pepper

2 Place the onions in a griddle pan and cook for 2–3 minutes. Now add the mushrooms and cook for a further 2 minutes until the onions and mushrooms are slightly blackened. Sprinkle with a little balsamic vinegar, salt and black pepper and cook for a further 2–3 minutes. Leave to cool and sprinkle over the pastry base.

225g/8oz cherry tomatoes – halved
225g/8oz fresh spinach
2 spring onions – chopped
110g/4oz low fat mozzarella cheese – cut into slices

3 Add the tomatoes, uncooked, to the pastry base, on top of the onions. Next add the spinach and sprinkle the spring onions on top. Arrange the cheese over the spinach.

570mls/1pt natural yoghurt
1 tsp paprika
3 eggs – lightly beaten
salt and freshly ground black pepper
110g/4oz low fat mozzarella cheese – grated

4 Mix the yoghurt, paprika, eggs, salt and black pepper until smooth, then pour over the top of the tart. Sprinkle with cheese.

lattice

6–8 slices of streaky bacon

5 Layer a few streaks of bacon on top and bake in the oven @ 190°C/gas mark 5 for 25–30 minutes or until cooked. Make sure the oven temperature is no higher, otherwise the yoghurt loses its texture and spoils.

hot spicy beef
with tortilla chips

Serves 4–6

This dish is quick and easy and ideal for those with a busy lifestyle. I use a similar cut of beef as I would for a stew yet this recipe radically reduces the cooking time from 2 hours to 10–15 minutes. The addition of a few spices and tortilla chips gives this dish a Mexican feel.

juice of 2 limes
juice of 1 lemon
2 dsp balsamic vinegar
$1/2$ tsp olive oil
700g/1$1/2$lbs chump steak – cut into wafer thin slices

1   Combine the juices and vinegar in a bowl to form a marinade. Cut the beef into wafer thin slices and place in the marinade for about 10 minutes.

2   Heat $1/2$ tsp oil in a non-stick wok. Add all the meat a little at a time keeping the temperature high and stir-fry continuously. This cooking should take approximately 7–8 minutes until all the liquid from the marinade has almost disappeared.

225g/8oz mushrooms – sliced

3   Add the mushrooms and cook for a further 2 minutes.

1 dsp chilli sauce
3–4 dsp tomato paste
1 spring onion – chopped
150mls/$1/4$pt vegetable stock

4   Add the chilli sauce, tomato paste and spring onion and cook thoroughly for 2–3 minutes. If you find the dish is drying out add a little stock.

fresh salad leaves
tortilla chips

Garnish with fresh salad leaves and serve with tortilla chips.

beef cooked the italian way

Serves 6

Beef cooked the Italian way is rich and tasty and made with garlic, herbs and red wine. This dish works best when the meat is allowed to soak in the marinade for as long as possible – up to twenty-four hours.

900g/2lbs chump steak
2 cloves of garlic – chopped
4 dsp balsamic vinegar
2 dsp honey

1 Cut the meat into strips and leave to marinate in the garlic, vinegar and honey for at least 30 minutes.

1 dsp olive oil

2 Drain the meat from the marinade and add to the hot oil in the pan. Cook over a high heat for 10–15 minutes until the meat becomes crispy and is almost cooked. Pour over the remainder of the marinade.

225g/8oz cherry tomatoes
110g/4oz black olives – stoned
150mls/¼pt passata
150mls/¼pt red wine

3 Add the tomatoes, black olives, passata and red wine to the pan. Simmer gently for 4–5 minutes until the sauce thickens. If you prefer more sauce add a little more passata and red wine.

handful of basil or flat leaf parsley – chopped
salt and freshly ground black pepper

4 Finally, add the basil. Heat through, season, and serve. I like this dish served with crusty bread or with a mixture of oven roasted vegetables such as aubergines, peppers and courgettes.

55

mediterranean vegetables and spicy beef

Serves 4

Mince steak is always convenient and just because we want a healthier diet, it doesn't mean we have to give up meat. Today, animals are fed on lower fat diets, which in turn provide us with leaner meat and protein products that are much healthier.

700g/1 1/2lbs lean mince beef

1 Cook the mince steak in a preheated non-stick pan without any oil for 2–3 minutes. Stir continuously as this will help to break down the meat.

1 red onion – 1/2 diced, 1/2 sliced
1 clove of garlic – sliced

2 Add the garlic and onion and simmer over a low heat for 5 minutes until the onion has softened slightly.

1 aubergine – cut into chunks
1 courgette – sliced

3 Add the aubergine and the courgette to the lightly cooked mince.

225g/8oz cherry tomatoes
110g/4oz sun blush tomatoes
few black/green olives
150mls/1/4pt passata
150mls/1/4pt vegetable stock

4 In quick succession, add the tomatoes, olives, passata and vegetable stock and mix well. Leave to simmer gently for 25–30 minutes.

1 bag assorted lettuce leaves
1 crusty loaf

Serve with a tossed green salad, a low fat dressing and some crusty bread. Alternatively, top with mozzarella cheese and brown under a hot grill. For a more filling meal, serve with low fat oven chips.

oil free tomato dressing

1 dsp passata
some torn basil leaves
1 tsp crushed garlic
1 tsp white wine vinegar
1 dsp honey
salt and freshly ground black pepper

Whisk all the ingredients together in a bowl until light and frothy. Season with salt and pepper.

middle eastern curry

Serves 4

This hearty curry is an economical one-pot dish made with beef, onions and potatoes, preferably of the waxy variety. It is quick and easy to cook and is perfect for eating on cold winter evenings.

450g/1lb steak pieces
1 tsp oil

1 Add the steak pieces and the oil to a very hot pan and toss over a high temperature for 4–5 minutes until the meat is browned.

2 tsp curry paste
1 dsp Worcester sauce

2 Add the curry paste and dry fry with the meat for 1 minute to intensify the flavour. Add the Worcester sauce and stir.

1 large onion – cut into rings
4–5 potatoes – diced
2 dsp onion relish
400g/14oz can of peach slices

3 Next in with the onions and potatoes and cook for several minutes. Add the relish, tinned peaches and juice and, again, mix well.

400g/14oz can of coconut milk

4 Finally, add the coconut milk – this will give a creaminess to the curry. Place the lid on the pan and leave to simmer very gently for 45 minutes to 1 hour until the meat is tender. It is important to stir the curry at regular intervals.

2 spring onions – finely chopped

5 Just before serving, add the spring onions. Cook for a further 2 minutes. Serve with poppadoms.

pork sausages with a
mustard and red onion gravy

Serves 4

Sausages make a delicious economical family meal if you add a little flavour and texture with a tasty mustard and onion gravy.

450g/1lb pork sausages – low fat
1 tsp olive oil
knob of butter

1. To cook the sausages, place in a hot pan with the olive oil and butter. Toss until golden and lightly cooked.

1 red onion – sliced
25g/1oz soft brown sugar

2. Add the sliced onion to the pan and cook until soft. Next, add the brown sugar and stir well to prevent it sticking.

1 dsp white wine vinegar
2 dsp Worcester sauce
125mls/4fl.oz vegetable stock

3. Now, in with the vinegar, Worcester sauce and vegetable stock. Continue cooking for 15–20 minutes until the sausages are well cooked and the onion gravy has reduced and concentrated in flavour.

1 tsp wholegrain mustard

4. Finally, add the mustard and heat through.

61

pork chops with peaches and parsley

Serves 4

This is a great way to cook pork chops so that they retain both their succulence and flavour. It is ideal for a family situation where everyone comes home at different times and expects a meal on the table in minutes.

4 loin pork chops
1 dsp olive oil

1 Place the pork chops into a hot roasting dish with a little oil. Brown on both sides.

1 dsp balsamic vinegar

2 Pour the balsamic vinegar over the chops.

1 red onion – cut into chunks
1 white onion – cut into chunks
3 stalks of celery – cut into chunks
225g/8oz tin of peach halves and juice

3 Scatter the onions and celery over the chops. Now add the tinned peaches and juice, mixing the ingredients in the roasting dish well.

6 potatoes – unpeeled and cut into wedges
275mls/^{1}/2pt vegetable stock
handful of parsley – finely chopped

4 Grill the potato wedges until the skin is crispy and brown and then add to the roasting dish. Pour over the stock and roast in the oven @ 200°C/gas mark 6 for 1–1^1/2 hours until the vegetables are cooked and the pork is tender. Garnish with parsley.

sticky pork ribs
with grilled potato wedges

Serves 6

A marinade will only do what you let it. If given enough time, it will work magic with even the humblest ingredients. I find it a good idea to make a little extra marinade as it can be reserved and used as a sauce.

450g/16oz tin of chopped tomatoes
75g/3oz muscovado sugar
2 cloves of garlic – chopped
1 tsp chilli sauce
1 dsp cider vinegar
1 dsp Worcester sauce
1 tsp paprika
salt and freshly ground black pepper

1 Pour all the marinade ingredients into a saucepan. Bring to the boil and cook for 5–6 minutes until the sugar has dissolved and the marinade has thickened.

900g /2lbs pork spare ribs

2 Pork ribs should require no preparation but if you are really watching the fat content of food, then you can cook them for 10–15 minutes in fast boiling water to remove most of the fat. Take the chops out of the pot, dry well and arrange in a roasting dish. Pour over the marinade and cook @ 200°C/gas mark 6 for 1 1/2 hours, basting regularly during cooking time.

grilled potato wedges

3–4 unpeeled potatoes steamed for 8–10 minutes
1 dsp olive oil
1 spring onion – chopped

3 Cut the potatoes into wedges after steaming and place in an ovenproof serving dish under the grill. Sprinkle with olive oil and grill for 4–5 minutes until crispy and golden. Serve garnished with spring onions. Pre-packed potato wedges can also be used and reheated in the same way.

pork chops – butterfly style
with peach chutney

Serves 2

Pork is a meat which I feel really improves if it has a chance to marinate. This is because it tends to dry out quite quickly during cooking.

2 pork chops – butterflied

1 Ask your butcher for 2 pork chops with little visible fat and ask him to butterfly them for you – this requires making an incision lengthways into the chop so that it can be opened out. Its shape resembles a butterfly.

2 dsp balsamic vinegar
2 dsp olive oil
1 dsp honey

2 Mix all the ingredients together to make the marinade. Pour over the pork chops, cover and leave to sit for at least 30 minutes.

3 Drain the chops and place in a hot pan. Cook until golden brown on both sides. Add the marinade a little at a time and leave the pork to cook for at least 25 minutes. Pork is one meat that needs to be cooked right through.

peach chutney

Chutneys have become very popular. Gone are the days when tomatoes and onions were the main ingredients. This chutney is hot, spicy and full of flavour.

4 peaches – diced
1/2 tsp chilli flakes
1 onion – chopped
1 inch of root ginger – finely chopped
110g/4oz soft brown sugar
4 dsp white wine vinegar
150mls/1/4pt orange juice

Put all the ingredients into a large saucepan. Bring to the boil, stirring continuously. Reduce the temperature and simmer with the lid on for 25 minutes. The texture of the chutney will change considerably. Serve as an accompaniment to the pork chops.

pepper crusted leg of lamb
with plum spiced cabbage

Serves 8

Roasting a leg of lamb the traditional way can take a couple of hours. In this recipe the bone is removed from the lamb and a few slits made in the open leg (your butcher will do this for you). This radically reduces the cooking time and allows you to flavour the lamb more thoroughly.

5lbs (approx) leg of lamb
1 dsp olive oil
1 dsp soy sauce
1/2 tsp salt

1 Flatten out the leg of lamb then pour over the olive oil, soy sauce and sprinkle with salt.

3–4 dsp peppercorns – crushed
2 dsp honey

2 Scatter the peppercorns over the lamb. Pat down well then drizzle with honey.

3 Place the lamb on a hot griddle pan and cook for 5 minutes on each side until golden and the flavours are well sealed in.

4 Continue by cooking the lamb in the oven @ 220°C/gas mark 7 for a further 45 minutes or until cooked to your taste.

225g/8oz baby potatoes

5 Roast the potatoes with the lamb in the oven.

plum spiced cabbage

A tasty plum sauce is a healthy way to spice up cabbage.

1 savoy cabbage – shredded

1 Shred and steam the cabbage for 4–5 minutes until cooked but still crunchy.

2 dsp plum sauce

2 Heat the plum sauce in a saucepan. Place the cabbage in a serving dish and pour over the plum sauce.

oven roasted lamb shanks
with oven roasted vegetables

Serves 4

Lamb shanks can either be taken from the shoulder or, for a meatier cut, from the leg. This cut of meat is tasty and cheap and when cooked with oven roasted vegetables makes an economic dish for all the family.

4 lamb shanks
4 cloves of garlic – paper on

225g/8oz baby onions – peeled
handful of sprigs of thyme
275mls/1/2pt vegetable stock
2 dsp redcurrant jelly (optional)

1   Place the lamb shanks in a large roasting dish and add the cloves of garlic.

2   Add the onions, thyme and stock and cook in a pre-heated oven @ 190°C/gas mark 5 for 1 1/2–2 hours until tender.

3   The liquid can be thickened slightly by the adding the redcurrant jelly. This will give an excellent flavour to the stock.

oven roasted vegetables

900g/2lbs carrots
900g/2lbs parsnips
2 red onions
450g/1lb baby potatoes
2 dsp lemon juice
1 dsp soft brown sugar
1 dsp olive oil
2 dsp honey
salt and freshly ground black pepper

1   Peel and slice the carrots, parsnips and onions. These look better if you cut them into chunks of similar size. Cut the baby potatoes in half.

2   Mix the lemon juice, sugar, oil, honey and seasoning in a bowl.

3   Put all the vegetables into a roasting dish and coat with the mixture.

4   Cook in a preheated oven @ 190°C/gas mark 5 for 1 hour.

1 sprig of parsley

Garnish with parsley and serve.

71

on the sweet side

For me, there just has to be pudding. I still love the old favourites,
like rice pudding, but I've mixed it with egg white to lighten it and
added toasted almonds and malted chocolate; or an apple pie made
with a golden yellow crunchy topping and filled with spiced apples.
The light vanilla pancakes are just a dream, so light and fluffy they
simply melt in your mouth. If it's sheer indulgence you're after then
the sunken raspberry and chocolate cake is for you, though
there's always the banana and sozzled sultana tart . . .

Shopping for fruit with Sandra at the local fruit shop in Cullybackey

sunken raspberry and chocolate cake

Serves 6–8

This is a wonderful cake, dark and chewy in the centre and packed full of flavour, texture and fruit. I am using raspberries here but any soft summer fruit would do just as well.

50g/2oz good quality dark chocolate
110g/4oz butter

1 Melt the chocolate and butter in a bowl over a saucepan of warm water. Stir well and keep an eye on the temperature.

3 eggs
225g/8oz soft brown sugar

2 Beat the eggs and sugar in a large bowl until light and fluffy. There is a lot of sugar in this cake so don't expect the volume to be very high. I find it a good idea to beat the eggs with half of the sugar and when fluffy, fold in the remainder of the sugar.

3 When the chocolate and butter have cooled, fold in the egg mixture.

110g/4oz self-raising flour

4 Add the flour and mix lightly.

50g/2oz ground almonds
25g/1oz chocolate chips
50g/2oz raspberries

5 Add the ground almonds and give another quick mix. Quickly add the chocolate chips and raspberries. If using frozen raspberries, defrost before using and remove any excess juice. Mix well then transfer to a lined 20cm/8 cake tin, either round or square.

6 Bake in the oven on the middle shelf @ 180°C/gas mark 4 for 35–40 minutes. The cake should be firm and leave the sides of the tin when ready. Remove and leave to cool. When ready to serve dust with a little icing sugar.

4 dsp yoghurt or 1 scoop of ice cream
berries

Serve with ice cream or yoghurt and berries.

vanilla pancakes
with poached rhubarb and cinnamon

Serves 4–5

This is a simple recipe for pancakes that works a treat every time.

110g/4oz plain flour
1 tsp baking powder
25g/1oz caster sugar
pinch salt

1 Mix all the dry ingredients in a large bowl.

150mls/¼pt buttermilk
yolk of 1 large egg
25g/1oz softened butter
¼ tsp vanilla extract
2 egg whites

2 In another bowl combine the buttermilk, egg yolk, softened butter and vanilla extract. Then add to the dry ingredients and mix well to form a smooth batter. Whisk the egg whites until light and fluffy, then fold into the batter. Mix gently and leave the batter to settle for a few minutes before cooking.

25g/1oz butter
1 dsp icing sugar

3 Melt a little butter in a shallow frying pan. Add a large spoonful of batter to the hot frying pan. Cook for 1–2 minutes on each side until golden and cooked. Cool on a tray and dust with icing sugar.

poached rhubarb

150mls/¼pt water
25g/1oz sugar
½ tsp cinnamon powder
2 stalks rhubarb – cut into chunks
natural yoghurt

1 Mix the water, sugar and cinnamon in a saucepan. Bring to the boil then turn the temperature down.

2 Add the rhubarb to the sugar syrup and poach gently for 5–6 minutes until the fruit is tender and soft but still holding its shape. Cool slightly before serving on top of the pancakes with a spoonful of natural yoghurt.

hot grilled exotic fruit
with nutmeg and crème fraîche

Serves 1

A very simple idea which can be used with almost any fruit, but especially with some of the more exotic fruits now available. My favourites are tamarillos – which are known as 'tree tomatoes' and which taste rather like kiwi fruit – but you can use mangoes, pawpaw and peaches. In this instance, I have used nectarines.

2 nectarines
25g/1oz icing sugar

Cut the nectarines in half, remove the stone and dust with icing sugar. Leave to sit for 15 minutes. Dust again with more icing sugar and cook below a hot grill for 2–3 minutes until caramelised and softened.

1/2 tsp nutmeg
2 dsp crème fraîche

Serve hot with a sprinkling of nutmeg and some crème fraîche.

79

pistachio nut meringue
with gingered caramel oranges

Serves 6–8

This simple meringue becomes an exciting pudding with the addition of gingered caramel oranges and pistachio nuts. With its tangy orange flavours, this dessert is a must.

3 egg whites
150g/5oz natural cane sugar
25g/1oz chopped pistachio nuts

1 Beat the egg whites and half the sugar in a large bowl until light and fluffy. Mix well to give the meringue a light texture. Add the remainder of the sugar and mix lightly. Gently add the chopped pistachio nuts. Place a piece of parchment paper on a baking sheet and use a 23cm/9 inch plate to trace an outline. Transfer the mixture to the baking sheet, flatten out and, with a palette knife, form into the shape of the circle. Bake @140°C/gas mark 1 for 45 minutes to 1 hour.

orange curd

juice of 1 orange
zest of 1/2 orange
50g/2oz caster sugar
10g/1/2oz arrowroot – blended with
2 dsp cold water
2 eggs – lightly beaten
25g/1oz butter

2 Put the orange juice and zest into a saucepan. Add the sugar and arrowroot and blend well. Finally add the eggs and butter and stir the mixture over the lowest heat for approximately 5 minutes, until the mixture thickens and loses its 'eggy' flavour. Be careful not to overheat or the mixture will turn into scrambled egg!

1 dsp orange liqueur

3 Add the orange liqueur, stir, and leave to cool.

gingered caramel oranges

275mls/1/2pt water
225g/8oz sugar
2 dsp cold water
1 inch of root ginger – finely chopped

1 Heat the water and sugar in a saucepan until golden and bubbling. Add the water and the ginger.

2 oranges – unpeeled and sliced

2 Place the oranges on a baking tray and pour the sugar syrup over them. Leave the oranges to cool for approximately 2 hours, then place on a rack to dry the underside.

225g/8oz tub yoghurt

3 Place the cooled meringue on a plate. Pour over the orange curd and top with yoghurt and the gingered caramel oranges.

81

cornmeal apple pie

Serves 4–6

The Bramley apple is renowned for its flavour and texture. Best of all it is available all year round and is one of the cheaper fruits.

4–5 Bramley apples
juice of 1 lemon

25g/1oz butter
25g/1oz demerara sugar
150mls/¹/4pt orange juice
zest of 1 orange

25g/1oz sultanas

1 tsp cinnamon powder

1 Peel and core the apples and cut into large chunks. If you wish, toss them in a little lemon juice to prevent browning.

2 Melt the butter in a pan. Add the apples and cook gently. Add the demerara sugar, orange juice and zest and then toss around for 1–2 minutes.

3 Add the sultanas. These will plump up and change in texture.

4 Finally, add the cinnamon powder. Place the lid on top and leave it to simmer gently for 6–7 minutes. Do not allow to overcook or the apples will lose their texture and shape.

crumble

110g/4oz polenta
110g/4oz plain flour
110g/4oz softened butter
50g/2oz demerara sugar

1 Mix the polenta and the plain flour in a bowl. Add the butter, cut through and rub in coarsely. Now, add the demerara sugar and mix until the contents resemble a coarse crumble.

2 Place the caramelised apples in an ovenproof dish, 18–20cm/7–8 inches in diameter. Sprinkle the crumble over the apples and bake in the oven @ 190°C/gas mark 5 for 25–30 minutes until bubbling and golden. Serve hot with custard.

tip

The addition of 1dsp of low fat yoghurt to custard will improve the consistency and holding qualities of the custard. However, if heating up be careful not to boil the custard again or the yoghurt will separate.

jenny's toffee apple cake

Serves 4–6

An apple pie with a bit of a twist. The Bramley apples are lightly poached until they become golden. Be careful not to overcook them.

toffee apple topping

50g/2oz butter
50g/2oz soft brown sugar
1 dsp orange zest
2 dsp fresh orange juice
6 Bramley apples – peeled and cut into large wedges

1 Heat the butter and sugar in a non-stick frying pan.

2 Add the orange zest and juice and cook over a high temperature until bubbling gently. Add the apple wedges and cook until golden. Drain the apples from the toffee mixture and arrange in a lined springform cake tin 18–20cm/7–8 inches in diameter. Cook the remaining toffee mixture in the pan for another couple of minutes. Pour over the apples and leave to cool.

all-in-one sponge

110g/4oz softened butter
110g/4oz caster sugar
4 small eggs – whisked
175g/6oz self-raising flour
1 tsp baking powder
1 tsp orange zest
1 tsp cinnamon powder

Put all the ingredients into a baking bowl. Beat well for 1 1/2–2 minutes until smooth, then spoon the mixture over the top of the cooled toffee apples and flatten the top. Bake in the oven @ 190°C/gas mark 5 for 30–35 minutes or until the cake is firm and cooked. Turn the cake out to cool and serve hot or cold with yoghurt.

marvellous malted soufflé rice pudding

Serves 4–6

This is a new twist on an old favourite – rice pudding with a crunchy toasted topping and a malted flavour. Kids just love it.

1 litre milk – semi-skimmed or full cream
110g/4oz rice pudding grains
25g/1oz caster sugar
few drops vanilla extract

1 Heat the milk in a large heavy based saucepan. Add the rice pudding grains to the milk. Next, in with the sugar and the vanilla extract.

2 Bring to the boil, then reduce the heat and leave to simmer gently for approximately 1 hour until the rice grains have swollen and absorbed the liquid and have become thick and creamy.

3 egg whites
1 packet malted chocolate sweets

3 Beat the egg whites in a large bowl until light and fluffy. Gently crumble the chocolate sweets into the rice. Now add the egg. Mix lightly then transfer to a greased ovenproof dish.

25g/1oz flaked almonds

4 Sprinkle with flaked almonds and bake in the oven @ 220°C/ gas mark 7 for 10–12 minutes until the pudding has puffed up and the almonds are golden. To serve, dust with icing sugar.

banana and sozzled sultana tart

Serves 6–8

A slice of banana tart is, for me, sheer indulgence. This tart is truly delicious – the base is made with toasted oats or muesli and a few sozzled sultanas and the sliced bananas are topped with a fudge sauce and toasted pistachio nuts.

110g/4oz oats or muesli

1   Toast the oats or muesli in the oven @ 200°C/gas mark 6 for 10 minutes.

50g/2oz sultanas
2 dsp rum

2   Steep the sultanas in rum for 10 minutes until they absorb the liquid and become soft. Add the sultanas to the toasted oats and mix.

225g/8oz good quality dark chocolate
10g/¹/₂oz butter
2 dsp honey

3   Melt the chocolate in a bowl over a saucepan of boiling water. Add the butter and honey, oats and sultanas and mix. Transfer to a lightly greased 23cm/9 inch springform flan tin. Press down and leave to cool.

the sauce

50g/2oz soft brown sugar
200ml/7oz tin of Ideal milk or
coconut milk
1 dsp lime juice
1 dsp honey
1 tsp rum – optional

1   Place all the ingredients in a saucepan. Bring to the boil, reduce the temperature and simmer slowly until the sauce thickens and becomes golden brown. Be patient – this takes a bit of time. Add the rum if desired.

4–5 bananas – sliced
juice of 1 lemon

2   Toss the bananas in a little lemon juice, arrange them on top of the base and pour the sauce over. Leave to cool before serving.

pistachio nuts – chopped

3   Toast some pistachio nuts under a hot grill for a couple of minutes. Be careful not to burn them. Chop and sprinkle over the tart.

vanilla sponge pudding
with a red berry salsa

serves 6–8

A light sponge with lots of lovely berries makes a delicious low fat pudding. This recipe is easily adapted to suit the time of year – just use whatever seasonal fruits are available.

5 eggs
150g/5oz caster sugar

1 Beat the eggs and caster sugar together in a bowl until the mixture forms light and foamy peaks. This takes about 6 to 8 minutes.

150g/5oz sieved plain flour

2 Gradually add the flour – about one third at a time – folding gently with a metal spoon after each addition.

few drops of vanilla extract

3 Add the vanilla extract before carefully pouring the mixture into a 18–20cm/7–8 inches tin that has been lightly greased and dusted with caster sugar. Bake in a preheated oven @ 200°C/gas mark 6 for 15–20 minutes.

4 Turn out onto a cooling tray and when cool, decorate with set yoghurt or fromage frais and fruit.

red berry salsa

The word 'salsa' means sauce and this dish is usually served as an accompaniment. This red berry salsa is colourful, cool and refreshing. Feel free to use whatever berries are in season.

225g/8oz strawberries
110g/4oz blueberries
110g/4oz raspberries
110g/4oz cranberries

1 Chop the strawberries into large chunks. Mix with the blueberries, raspberries and cranberries.

1 dsp fresh orange juice
1 dsp icing sugar

2 Mix the orange juice and icing sugar and leave to sit for a few minutes before pouring over the fruit.

no cook corner

This section is for all those who feel they can't cook, don't cook or simply haven't time to cook! Often we have to turn out dishes that are tasty and full of goodness with very little time to hand. Let me show you how, with a little imagination and some wise shopping, you can produce stunning main courses and desserts – and make it look as though you have spent hours in the kitchen instead of minutes!

crispy beef with beans and noodles

serves 2

1 tsp olive oil
225g/8oz thinly sliced beef – cut into strips
packet of fresh sliced green beans
200g/7oz jar of black bean sauce
250g/9oz packet of egg noodles

Heat the oil in a wok or pan and add the sliced beef. Fry for 2–3 minutes. Now add the green beans and pour in the jar of black bean sauce. Simmer for about 10 minutes until everything is cooked. Meanwhile, boil the noodles until they are soft. This should only take a couple of minutes.

medley of stir-fried vegetables

serves 2

225g/8oz bag freezer rice
1 tsp olive oil
350g/12oz packet Chinese vegetables
6 dsp plum sauce
2 dsp soy sauce
parsley – chopped

Microwave the rice for 3 minutes on full power. Heat the oil in a wok or pan, add the vegetables and cook on a high heat for 2–3 minutes. Add the plum and soy sauce and heat thoroughly. Serve the vegetables on top of the rice and garnish with parsley.

tuna gnocchi

serves 4

250g/9oz packet of fresh gnocchi
1 tsp olive oil
pinch of salt
2 x 160g/5½oz tins of tuna fish
275g/10oz jar of good quality tomato sauce
sprig of basil

Put the oil and a pinch of salt into a saucepan of boiling water and add the gnocchi. Cook according to the instructions. Drain. In another pan place the tomato sauce and crumble in the tuna fish. Heat for 2 minutes until warmed through. Pour the tomato mixture over the gnocchi and garnish with a sprig of basil.

savoury tray bake

serves 4

1 large savoury tray base – e.g. pizza base
1 red onion
110g/4oz cherry tomatoes – halved
4–6 rashers of streaky bacon
110g/4oz cheddar or mozzarella cheese

If you have two or three children to feed at a moment's notice, then try this. Just take a ready-made savoury tray bake and add a few thin slices of red onion. Next add some cherry tomatoes and a few strips of streaky bacon. Finally crumble over a little cheese. Pop into the oven @ 200°C/gas mark 6 for 12–15 minutes. Serve with chips or salad.

berry baskets

serves 4

packet of wafer baskets or chocolate cups
110g/4oz of ice cream or yoghurt
450g/1lb of assorted fresh/frozen berries
jar of raspberry sauce or coulis
chocolate leaves   } to decorate
fresh mint

Arrange the baskets on a plate. Fill with ice cream and top with berries. Now pour over the raspberry coulis and decorate with chocolate leaves and fresh mint.

raspberry and almond pudding

serves 4–6

450g/1lb raspberries
570mls/1pt Greek yoghurt
225g/8oz almond biscuits – crushed
110g/4oz blueberries
1 passion fruit

Put half of the raspberries into a serving bowl. Top with a mixture of the yoghurt and crushed almond biscuits. Now add the other half of the raspberries and finish off with yoghurt topped with raspberries, blueberries and passion fruit.

layered sponge cake
with yoghurt and berried fruits

serves 6–8

3 sponge bases
200mls/6floz crème fraîche
200mls/6floz Greek yoghurt or mascarpone cheese
assorted fresh fruit

Mix the crème fraîche with the fruit and spread each base with the mixture. Stack the sponge bases carefully on top of each other. Now cover the entire cake with Greek yoghurt or mascarpone cheese and decorate with fresh fruit. Dust with icing sugar before serving.

tropical fruit pudding

serves 4–6

225g/8oz packet of sponge fingers
570mls/1pt carton of tropical fruit
200mls/6floz fromage frais
jar of toffee sauce

Place the sponge fingers in the bottom of a glass bowl. Pour in the toffee sauce and top with a mixture of fromage frais and tropical fruit.

kids corner

These simple recipes and ideas are mostly based on fruit and vegetables. They are great fun to try with your kids and will also encourage them to eat good healthy food from an early age. Hopefully the ideas here will also stimulate your children's interest in cooking and will help you and them to come up with a few recipes of your own. Have fun!

A word of warning – be careful not to use anything that could be a danger to the children such as cocktail sticks or other sharp objects. Use edible foods for decoration such as pasta, berries, sweets or some lightly cooked, softened beans. Be sure to check for allergies.

From left to right: Jasper, Marcus and George

exotic fruit face

Choose as many types and colours of fruit as you like and cut them into shapes. See who can make the **funniest** or the **saddest** or the **silliest** face.

The caterpillar is made very simply from pieces of kiwi fruit. Create your own animals from any fruit you like.

mango mouth strawberry nose kiwi eyes orange eyebrows pineapple and blueberry earri

tons of jelly

To make jelly add water to some jelly crystals or cubes. To make a mousse add milk instead of water. Serve in tall glasses or dessert bowls for a party feel.

green frog mousse sticky orange mousse wobbly strawberry jelly lazy lemon jelly

These strawberry faces have cranberries and blueberries for eyes.

green celery sticks orange carrot sticks yellow corn cobs

red peppers yellow peppers

dips and bites

Dip lots of vegetable pieces into
mayonnaise, cottage cheese,
fromage frais or natural yoghurt.

tomato soup tomato man cucumber boat with cheese and apple cubes

baked potato with lots of lovely fillings

Heat some tomato soup
and stir in a spoonful of
yoghurt. Place a leaf of basil in
the middle and eat the soup
with bread or pasta.

Make a boat out of cucumber and fill
it with cubes of cheese and apple.

Baked potatoes are yummy filled with
cottage cheese, coleslaw, baked beans
or anything you fancy.

101

acknowledgements

It takes the help, advice and patience of so very many people to coordinate a cookery series and a cookbook. So a big thank you to: Alan Bremner and Orla McKibbin at UTV for their enthusiasm in the development of *Gloriously Good Food* – the series and the book; Ruth Johnston, producer and director, and the crew who worked on all or part of the series, Blane Scott, P.J. McGirr, Liz Stewart, Ronnie Martin, Mary McCleave, Bill Rowan and Jimmy McConville; the photography team, Robert McKeag and Howard Ward; Colette Coughlan, the food stylist; the book team at Blackstaff Press, Wendy Dunbar, Patsy Horton, Bronagh McVeigh, Bairbre Ryan and Anne Tannahill; Maureen Best, Anna

Livingstone and Pauline Brennan for their hard work behind the scenes; hair stylist Donna McAleese at Peter Mark, Ballymena; Bertie McNeill; and Vera McCready for her help in typing up text.

Thanks are also due to Helen Turkington at the Fabric Library, Cookstown, Enniskillen and Newbridge, County Kildare, for her choice of fabrics and furnishings for the barn; Paddy McNeill of Beeswax, Kilrea for his help in sourcing all the free-standing dressers and cupboards; Sally at Floral Design, Ballymena, for the fresh flower arrangements; Nicholas Mosse Pottery, Kilkenny; Christine Foy, Mullaghmeen Pottery, Enniskillen; Michelle Kershaw and Diane at Lakeland Plastics; Habitat, Belfast; Laura Ashley, Belfast; Jemima at Prestige; Helen Bedford at Le Creuset; Hilary Robinson at Presence, Belfast, for cookware; Reagan Tiles; Madeline at Baumatic; Hewitt & Robinson; Redfyre Cookers; Maud Hamill at Calor Gas for all her coordination and help with appliances; BIK Distributors Limited, Belfast; Jim Glass, Thomas Boal, Joe McMullan, Charlie McCarrol and Ken Mooney who worked so hard at converting the barn into my new kitchen location.

index

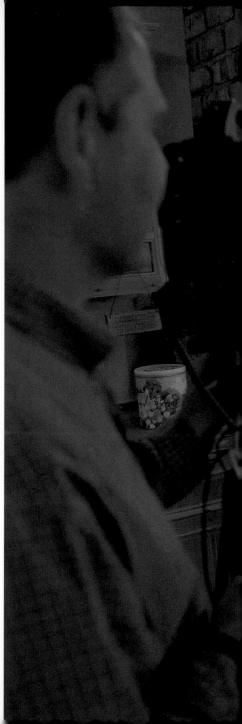

First published in 2001 by
The Blackstaff Press Limited,
Wildflower Way, Apollo Road,
Belfast BT12 6TA,
in association with UTV

Reprinted November 2001

Printed in Northern Ireland by W & G Baird Limited
A CIP catalogue record for this book
is available from the British Library

ISBN 0-86540-700-3

www.blackstaffpress.com